50 Irresistible Doughnuts to Make at Home

By: Kelly Johnson

Table of Contents

- Classic Glazed Doughnuts
- Chocolate Frosted Doughnuts
- Cinnamon Sugar Doughnuts
- Jelly-Filled Doughnuts
- Boston Cream Doughnuts
- Maple Glazed Doughnuts
- Old-Fashioned Doughnuts
- Blueberry Doughnuts
- Powdered Sugar Doughnuts
- Lemon Poppy Seed Doughnuts
- Red Velvet Doughnuts
- Pumpkin Spice Doughnuts
- Apple Cider Doughnuts
- Double Chocolate Doughnuts
- Strawberry Frosted Doughnuts
- Vanilla Bean Doughnuts
- Churro Doughnuts
- Caramel Glazed Doughnuts
- Nutella-Filled Doughnuts
- Peanut Butter Glazed Doughnuts
- S'mores Doughnuts
- Matcha Green Tea Doughnuts
- Coconut Cream Doughnuts
- Raspberry Glazed Doughnuts
- Cookies and Cream Doughnuts
- Funfetti Doughnuts
- Mocha Glazed Doughnuts
- Pistachio Doughnuts
- Mango Glazed Doughnuts
- Salted Caramel Doughnuts
- Tiramisu Doughnuts
- Banana Cream Doughnuts
- Almond Joy Doughnuts
- Spiced Chai Doughnuts
- Gingerbread Doughnuts

- White Chocolate Cranberry Doughnuts
- Honey Glazed Doughnuts
- Lavender Glazed Doughnuts
- Cardamom Sugar Doughnuts
- Chocolate Orange Doughnuts
- Black Forest Doughnuts
- Espresso Glazed Doughnuts
- Pear and Cinnamon Doughnuts
- Mango and Coconut Doughnuts
- Pineapple Upside-Down Doughnuts
- Bourbon Glazed Doughnuts
- Cheesecake Doughnuts
- Dulce de Leche Doughnuts
- Chocolate Mint Doughnuts
- Raspberry White Chocolate Doughnuts

Classic Glazed Doughnuts

Ingredients

For the Doughnuts:

- 3 ¼ cups all-purpose flour, plus extra for dusting
- 2 ¼ teaspoons (1 packet) active dry yeast
- ½ cup whole milk, warmed (110°F/43°C)
- ¼ cup granulated sugar
- 2 large eggs
- 4 tablespoons unsalted butter, softened
- ½ teaspoon salt
- ½ teaspoon vanilla extract
- Vegetable oil, for frying

For the Glaze:

- 2 cups powdered sugar
- ¼ cup whole milk
- 1 teaspoon vanilla extract

Instructions

1. Prepare the Dough:

- In a small bowl, combine warm milk and yeast. Let it sit for 5 minutes until frothy.
- In a large mixing bowl, combine flour, sugar, and salt. Add the yeast mixture, eggs, butter, and vanilla.
- Knead the dough on a floured surface for 8–10 minutes until smooth and elastic. Alternatively, use a stand mixer with a dough hook for 5–7 minutes.

2. Proof the Dough:

- Place the dough in a greased bowl, cover with a clean towel, and let it rise in a warm place for 1–2 hours, or until doubled in size.

3. Shape the Doughnuts:

- Roll the dough to about ½ inch thick on a floured surface. Use a doughnut cutter or two round cutters (3-inch and 1-inch) to shape the doughnuts.

- Place the doughnuts on a floured tray, cover, and let them rise for another 30–45 minutes until puffed.

4. Fry the Doughnuts:

- Heat 2–3 inches of oil in a heavy-bottomed pot to 350°F (175°C).
- Fry 2–3 doughnuts at a time, cooking for 1–2 minutes per side until golden brown.
- Remove with a slotted spoon and drain on a wire rack lined with paper towels.

5. Make the Glaze:

- In a bowl, whisk together powdered sugar, milk, and vanilla extract until smooth.

6. Glaze the Doughnuts:

- Dip each warm doughnut into the glaze, allowing the excess to drip off.
- Place the glazed doughnuts back on the wire rack for the glaze to set.

Chocolate Frosted Doughnuts

Ingredients

For the Doughnuts:

- Use the same doughnut recipe from the Classic Glazed Doughnuts above.

For the Chocolate Frosting:

- 1 ½ cups powdered sugar
- ¼ cup unsweetened cocoa powder
- ¼ cup whole milk
- 1 teaspoon vanilla extract
- Pinch of salt

Instructions

1. **Prepare and Fry the Doughnuts:**
   Follow the same instructions as the Classic Glazed Doughnuts for preparing, proofing, shaping, and frying the doughnuts.
2. **Make the Chocolate Frosting:**
   - In a bowl, whisk together powdered sugar, cocoa powder, milk, vanilla extract, and a pinch of salt until smooth. Adjust the milk for desired consistency.
3. **Frost the Doughnuts:**
   - Once the fried doughnuts have cooled slightly, dip the tops into the chocolate frosting.
   - Let the frosting set on a wire rack before serving.

Cinnamon Sugar Doughnuts

Ingredients

For the Doughnuts:

- Use the same doughnut recipe from the Classic Glazed Doughnuts above.

For the Cinnamon Sugar Coating:

- 1 cup granulated sugar
- 2 teaspoons ground cinnamon

Instructions

1. **Prepare and Fry the Doughnuts:**
   Follow the same instructions as the Classic Glazed Doughnuts for preparing, proofing, shaping, and frying the doughnuts.
2. **Make the Cinnamon Sugar Coating:**
   - In a shallow dish, mix granulated sugar and cinnamon until well combined.
3. **Coat the Doughnuts:**
   - While the doughnuts are still warm, roll them in the cinnamon sugar mixture until fully coated.

Jelly-Filled Doughnuts

Ingredients

For the Doughnuts:

- Use the same doughnut recipe from the Classic Glazed Doughnuts above.

For the Filling:

- 1 cup jelly or jam of your choice (strawberry, raspberry, or grape work well)
- Powdered sugar (optional, for dusting)

Instructions

1. **Prepare and Fry the Doughnuts:**
   - Follow the same instructions as the Classic Glazed Doughnuts for preparing, proofing, and frying the doughnuts.
   - Instead of cutting a hole in the middle, keep the doughnut rounds whole.
2. **Fill the Doughnuts:**
   - Once the doughnuts are cool enough to handle, use a piping bag fitted with a small round tip.
   - Insert the tip into the side of each doughnut and fill it with your choice of jelly or jam.
3. **Optional Topping:**
   - Dust the tops of the filled doughnuts with powdered sugar for a classic finish.

Boston Cream Doughnuts

Ingredients

For the Pastry Cream:

- 1 ½ cups whole milk
- ½ cup granulated sugar
- 3 large egg yolks
- 3 tablespoons cornstarch
- 2 tablespoons unsalted butter
- 1 teaspoon vanilla extract

For the Chocolate Glaze:

- 1 cup semi-sweet chocolate chips
- ½ cup heavy cream

Instructions

1. **Prepare and Fry Doughnuts:**
   Follow the Classic Doughnut recipe, keeping the dough rounds whole (no hole in the center).
2. **Make the Pastry Cream:**
   - Heat milk in a saucepan until warm.
   - In a bowl, whisk sugar, egg yolks, and cornstarch. Gradually whisk in warm milk.
   - Return to heat and cook until thickened, stirring constantly.
   - Remove from heat, stir in butter and vanilla, and chill.
3. **Fill Doughnuts:**
   Use a piping bag with a small tip to fill the cooled doughnuts with pastry cream.
4. **Prepare the Chocolate Glaze:**
   Heat heavy cream and pour over chocolate chips. Let sit, then whisk until smooth.
5. **Assemble:**
   Dip the tops of filled doughnuts in the chocolate glaze.

Maple Glazed Doughnuts

Ingredients

For the Maple Glaze:

- 2 cups powdered sugar
- ¼ cup maple syrup
- 2 tablespoons milk

Instructions

1. **Prepare and Fry Doughnuts:**
   Follow the Classic Doughnut recipe.
2. **Make the Maple Glaze:**
   Mix powdered sugar, maple syrup, and milk until smooth.
3. **Glaze Doughnuts:**
   Dip warm doughnuts into the glaze and let set on a wire rack.

Old-Fashioned Doughnuts

Ingredients

- Use the Classic Doughnut recipe but roll the dough slightly thicker (¾ inch) and cut with a doughnut cutter.

Instructions

1. Fry doughnuts at 325°F (163°C) for a slightly crispier exterior.
2. Dip in vanilla glaze or leave plain.

Blueberry Doughnuts

Ingredients

- ½ cup fresh or frozen blueberries, mashed
- Add to Classic Doughnut batter during mixing.

Instructions

1. Prepare, fry, and glaze as desired (vanilla glaze pairs well).

Powdered Sugar Doughnuts

Ingredients

- 1 cup powdered sugar

Instructions

1. Roll warm doughnuts in powdered sugar until fully coated.

Lemon Poppy Seed Doughnuts

Ingredients

- Add 1 tablespoon lemon zest and 1 tablespoon poppy seeds to the Classic Doughnut batter.

Instructions

1. Prepare and fry doughnuts.
2. Top with lemon glaze (powdered sugar, lemon juice, and milk).

Red Velvet Doughnuts

Ingredients

- Add 2 tablespoons cocoa powder and 1 teaspoon red food coloring to the Classic Doughnut batter.

Instructions

1. Prepare, fry, and glaze with cream cheese frosting (softened cream cheese, powdered sugar, and milk).

Pumpkin Spice Doughnuts

Ingredients

- Replace ½ cup milk with ½ cup canned pumpkin puree.
- Add 1 teaspoon pumpkin spice to the dough.

Instructions

1. Fry and coat with cinnamon sugar or vanilla glaze.

Apple Cider Doughnuts

Ingredients

- Reduce 1 cup apple cider to ½ cup and use instead of milk.
- Add 1 teaspoon cinnamon and ½ teaspoon nutmeg to the dough.

Instructions

1. Fry and coat with cinnamon sugar.

Double Chocolate Doughnuts

Ingredients

- Add ¼ cup cocoa powder to the dough.

For the Glaze:

- 1 cup powdered sugar
- ¼ cup unsweetened cocoa powder
- 2 tablespoons milk

Instructions

1. Prepare, fry, and glaze with the chocolate glaze.

Strawberry Frosted Doughnuts

Ingredients

For the Frosting:

- 1 cup powdered sugar
- 2-3 tablespoons pureed strawberries

Instructions

1. Prepare and fry doughnuts.
2. Dip in strawberry frosting and top with sprinkles if desired.

Vanilla Bean Doughnuts

Ingredients

For the Glaze:

- 2 cups powdered sugar
- 3 tablespoons whole milk
- 1 vanilla bean, seeds scraped (or 1 teaspoon vanilla bean paste)

Instructions

1. **Prepare and Fry Doughnuts:**
   Follow the Classic Doughnut recipe.
2. **Make the Glaze:**
   Mix powdered sugar, milk, and vanilla bean seeds until smooth.
3. **Glaze Doughnuts:**
   Dip warm doughnuts into the vanilla bean glaze and let set.

Churro Doughnuts

Ingredients

For the Coating:

- 1 cup granulated sugar
- 2 teaspoons ground cinnamon

Instructions

1. **Prepare and Fry Doughnuts:**
   Follow the Classic Doughnut recipe, shaping them as long strips or twists if desired.
2. **Coat Doughnuts:**
   Roll warm doughnuts in the cinnamon-sugar mixture.

Caramel Glazed Doughnuts

Ingredients

For the Glaze:

- 1 cup granulated sugar
- 4 tablespoons unsalted butter
- ½ cup heavy cream

Instructions

1. **Prepare and Fry Doughnuts:**
   Follow the Classic Doughnut recipe.
2. **Make the Caramel Glaze:**
   - Melt sugar in a saucepan until golden brown.
   - Stir in butter and heavy cream until smooth.
3. **Glaze Doughnuts:**
   Dip the tops of the doughnuts into the warm caramel glaze.

Nutella-Filled Doughnuts

Ingredients

- 1 cup Nutella

Instructions

1. **Prepare and Fry Doughnuts:**
   Keep doughnuts whole (no center hole).
2. **Fill Doughnuts:**
   Use a piping bag with a small round tip to fill each doughnut with Nutella.
3. **Optional Topping:**
   Dust with powdered sugar or drizzle Nutella on top.

Peanut Butter Glazed Doughnuts

Ingredients

For the Glaze:

- 1 cup powdered sugar
- 2 tablespoons creamy peanut butter
- 2–3 tablespoons milk

Instructions

1. **Prepare and Fry Doughnuts:**
   Follow the Classic Doughnut recipe.
2. **Make the Glaze:**
   Mix powdered sugar, peanut butter, and milk until smooth.
3. **Glaze Doughnuts:**
   Dip doughnuts into the peanut butter glaze and let set.

S'mores Doughnuts

Ingredients

- ½ cup crushed graham crackers
- 1 cup mini marshmallows
- 1 cup melted chocolate

Instructions

1. **Prepare and Fry Doughnuts:**
   Follow the Classic Doughnut recipe.
2. **Assemble S'mores Topping:**
   - Dip doughnuts in melted chocolate.
   - Sprinkle with graham crackers and top with mini marshmallows.
3. **Toast Marshmallows:**
   Lightly toast marshmallows with a kitchen torch if desired.

Matcha Green Tea Doughnuts

Ingredients

For the Glaze:

- 2 cups powdered sugar
- 2 tablespoons matcha powder
- 3–4 tablespoons milk

Instructions

1. **Prepare and Fry Doughnuts:**
   Follow the Classic Doughnut recipe.
2. **Make the Matcha Glaze:**
   Mix powdered sugar, matcha powder, and milk until smooth.
3. **Glaze Doughnuts:**
   Dip doughnuts in the matcha glaze and let set.

Coconut Cream Doughnuts

Ingredients

- 1 cup coconut cream or whipped coconut cream
- ½ cup shredded coconut (toasted, optional)

Instructions

1. **Prepare and Fry Doughnuts:**
   Follow the Classic Doughnut recipe.
2. **Fill Doughnuts:**
   Use a piping bag to fill doughnuts with coconut cream.
3. **Top Doughnuts:**
   Sprinkle with toasted shredded coconut.

Raspberry Glazed Doughnuts

Ingredients

For the Glaze:

- 1 cup powdered sugar
- 3 tablespoons raspberry puree

Instructions

1. **Prepare and Fry Doughnuts:**
   Follow the Classic Doughnut recipe.
2. **Make the Raspberry Glaze:**
   Mix powdered sugar and raspberry puree until smooth.
3. **Glaze Doughnuts:**
   Dip warm doughnuts into the raspberry glaze.

Cookies and Cream Doughnuts

Ingredients

- ½ cup crushed chocolate sandwich cookies (e.g., Oreos)
  For the Glaze:
- 1 cup powdered sugar
- 2 tablespoons milk
- 1 teaspoon vanilla extract

Instructions

1. **Prepare and Fry Doughnuts:**
   Follow the Classic Doughnut recipe.
2. **Make the Glaze:**
   Mix powdered sugar, milk, and vanilla extract.
3. **Top Doughnuts:**
   Dip doughnuts in the glaze and sprinkle with crushed cookies.

Funfetti Doughnuts

Ingredients

- 2 tablespoons rainbow sprinkles (mixed into the dough)
  For the Glaze:
- 1 cup powdered sugar
- 2 tablespoons milk
- Additional sprinkles for topping

Instructions

1. **Prepare and Fry Doughnuts:**
   Mix sprinkles into the dough before shaping.
2. **Make the Glaze:**
   Mix powdered sugar and milk until smooth.
3. **Glaze Doughnuts:**
   Dip doughnuts in the glaze and top with extra sprinkles.

Mocha Glazed Doughnuts

Ingredients

For the Glaze:

- 1 cup powdered sugar
- 2 tablespoons brewed espresso (cooled)
- 2 tablespoons cocoa powder

Instructions

1. **Prepare and Fry Doughnuts:**
   Follow the Classic Doughnut recipe.
2. **Make the Mocha Glaze:**
   Whisk powdered sugar, espresso, and cocoa powder until smooth.
3. **Glaze Doughnuts:**
   Dip doughnuts into the mocha glaze and let set.

Pistachio Doughnuts

Ingredients

- ½ cup finely chopped pistachios
  For the Glaze:
- 1 cup powdered sugar
- 3 tablespoons milk
- 1 teaspoon almond extract

Instructions

1. **Prepare and Fry Doughnuts:**
   Follow the Classic Doughnut recipe.
2. **Make the Glaze:**
   Mix powdered sugar, milk, and almond extract.
3. **Top Doughnuts:**
   Dip in the glaze and sprinkle with chopped pistachios.

Mango Glazed Doughnuts

Ingredients

For the Glaze:

- 1 cup powdered sugar
- 3 tablespoons mango puree
- 1 teaspoon lime juice

Instructions

1. **Prepare and Fry Doughnuts:**
   Follow the Classic Doughnut recipe.
2. **Make the Mango Glaze:**
   Combine powdered sugar, mango puree, and lime juice until smooth.
3. **Glaze Doughnuts:**
   Dip warm doughnuts into the mango glaze and let set.

Salted Caramel Doughnuts

Ingredients

For the Glaze:

- 1 cup granulated sugar
- 4 tablespoons butter
- ½ cup heavy cream
- 1 teaspoon sea salt

Instructions

1. **Prepare and Fry Doughnuts:**
   Follow the Classic Doughnut recipe.
2. **Make the Caramel Glaze:**
   Melt sugar in a saucepan until golden. Add butter, cream, and salt. Stir until smooth.
3. **Glaze Doughnuts:**
   Dip the tops of doughnuts in warm caramel glaze.

Tiramisu Doughnuts

Ingredients

For Filling:

- 1 cup mascarpone cheese
- ½ cup powdered sugar
- 2 tablespoons brewed espresso

For Topping:

- Cocoa powder

Instructions

1. **Prepare and Fry Doughnuts:**
   Use whole doughnuts (no hole).
2. **Fill Doughnuts:**
   Mix mascarpone, powdered sugar, and espresso. Pipe filling into doughnuts.
3. **Top Doughnuts:**
   Dust tops with cocoa powder.

Banana Cream Doughnuts

Ingredients

For Filling:

- 1 cup banana pudding
- ½ cup whipped cream

Instructions

1. **Prepare and Fry Doughnuts:**
   Use whole doughnuts (no hole).
2. **Fill Doughnuts:**
   Pipe banana pudding into the doughnuts.
3. **Top Doughnuts:**
   Dust with powdered sugar or drizzle with chocolate.

Almond Joy Doughnuts

Ingredients

For Topping:

- ½ cup shredded coconut (toasted)
- ¼ cup chopped almonds
- 1 cup melted chocolate

Instructions

1. **Prepare and Fry Doughnuts:**
   Follow the Classic Doughnut recipe.
2. **Assemble Toppings:**
   Dip doughnuts in melted chocolate. Sprinkle with toasted coconut and chopped almonds.

Spiced Chai Doughnuts

Ingredients

For the Glaze:

- 1 cup powdered sugar
- 3 tablespoons brewed chai tea (cooled)
- ½ teaspoon cinnamon

Instructions

1. **Prepare and Fry Doughnuts:**
   Follow the Classic Doughnut recipe.
2. **Make the Chai Glaze:**
   Mix powdered sugar, chai tea, and cinnamon until smooth.
3. **Glaze Doughnuts:**
   Dip warm doughnuts into the chai glaze.

Gingerbread Doughnuts

Ingredients

For the Dough:

- Add 1 teaspoon ground ginger and 1 teaspoon ground cinnamon to the dough.

For the Glaze:

- 1 cup powdered sugar
- 2 tablespoons molasses
- 2 tablespoons milk

Instructions

1. **Prepare and Fry Doughnuts:**
   Mix spices into the dough. Fry as usual.
2. **Make the Glaze:**
   Combine powdered sugar, molasses, and milk until smooth.
3. **Glaze Doughnuts:**
   Dip doughnuts in the glaze and let set.

White Chocolate Cranberry Doughnuts

Ingredients

For the Topping:

- ½ cup dried cranberries
- 1 cup melted white chocolate

Instructions

1. **Prepare and Fry Doughnuts:**
   Follow the Classic Doughnut recipe.
2. **Top Doughnuts:**
   Dip doughnuts in melted white chocolate and sprinkle with dried cranberries.

Honey Glazed Doughnuts

Ingredients

For the Glaze:

- ½ cup honey
- 2 tablespoons butter
- 1 cup powdered sugar
- 2 tablespoons whole milk

Instructions

1. **Prepare and Fry Doughnuts:**
   Follow the Classic Doughnut recipe.
2. **Make the Honey Glaze:**
   In a saucepan, melt honey and butter. Stir in powdered sugar and milk until smooth.
3. **Glaze Doughnuts:**
   Dip warm doughnuts into the honey glaze and let set.

Lavender Glazed Doughnuts

Ingredients

For the Glaze:

- 1 cup powdered sugar
- 2 tablespoons milk
- 1 tablespoon dried lavender buds (finely ground)

Instructions

1. **Prepare and Fry Doughnuts:**
   Follow the Classic Doughnut recipe.
2. **Make the Lavender Glaze:**
   Whisk powdered sugar, milk, and ground lavender until smooth.
3. **Glaze Doughnuts:**
   Dip doughnuts into the lavender glaze and allow it to set.

Cardamom Sugar Doughnuts

Ingredients

For the Sugar Coating:

- ½ cup granulated sugar
- 1 tablespoon ground cardamom

Instructions

1. **Prepare and Fry Doughnuts:**
   Follow the Classic Doughnut recipe.
2. **Make the Sugar Coating:**
   Combine granulated sugar and ground cardamom.
3. **Coat Doughnuts:**
   While still warm, roll doughnuts in the cardamom sugar mixture.

Chocolate Orange Doughnuts

Ingredients

For the Glaze:

- 1 cup powdered sugar
- 2 tablespoons cocoa powder
- 2 tablespoons orange juice
- ½ teaspoon orange zest

Instructions

1. **Prepare and Fry Doughnuts:**
   Follow the Classic Doughnut recipe.
2. **Make the Chocolate Orange Glaze:**
   Whisk powdered sugar, cocoa powder, orange juice, and orange zest until smooth.
3. **Glaze Doughnuts:**
   Dip doughnuts into the chocolate orange glaze and let set.

Black Forest Doughnuts

Ingredients

For the Filling:

- 1 cup whipped cream
- 1 cup cherry preserves

For the Topping:

- 1 cup dark chocolate ganache

Instructions

1. **Prepare and Fry Doughnuts:**
   Follow the Classic Doughnut recipe.
2. **Fill Doughnuts:**
   Use a piping bag to fill doughnuts with whipped cream and cherry preserves.
3. **Top with Ganache:**
   Drizzle dark chocolate ganache over the top of each doughnut.

Espresso Glazed Doughnuts

Ingredients

For the Glaze:

- 1 cup powdered sugar
- 2 tablespoons brewed espresso (cooled)
- 1 tablespoon heavy cream

Instructions

1. **Prepare and Fry Doughnuts:**
   Follow the Classic Doughnut recipe.
2. **Make the Espresso Glaze:**
   Whisk powdered sugar, espresso, and heavy cream until smooth.
3. **Glaze Doughnuts:**
   Dip doughnuts into the espresso glaze and allow it to set.

Pear and Cinnamon Doughnuts

Ingredients

For the Glaze:

- 1 cup powdered sugar
- 3 tablespoons pear juice or pear puree
- ½ teaspoon ground cinnamon

Instructions

1. **Prepare and Fry Doughnuts:**
   Follow the Classic Doughnut recipe.
2. **Make the Pear and Cinnamon Glaze:**
   Whisk powdered sugar, pear juice, and ground cinnamon until smooth.
3. **Glaze Doughnuts:**
   Dip doughnuts into the pear and cinnamon glaze and let set.

Mango and Coconut Doughnuts

Ingredients

For the Glaze:

- 1 cup powdered sugar
- 3 tablespoons mango puree
- 1 teaspoon coconut extract

For the Topping:

- ½ cup shredded coconut (toasted)

Instructions

1. **Prepare and Fry Doughnuts:**
   Follow the Classic Doughnut recipe.
2. **Make the Mango Coconut Glaze:**
   Whisk powdered sugar, mango puree, and coconut extract until smooth.
3. **Glaze Doughnuts:**
   Dip doughnuts in the glaze and sprinkle with toasted shredded coconut.

Pineapple Upside-Down Doughnuts

Ingredients

For the Topping:

- ½ cup brown sugar
- 2 tablespoons unsalted butter
- ½ cup diced pineapple (fresh or canned)
- Maraschino cherries (optional)

Instructions

1. **Prepare and Fry Doughnuts:**
   Follow the Classic Doughnut recipe, but use a doughnut pan for a shaped version.
2. **Prepare Pineapple Topping:**
   Melt butter in a pan, add brown sugar, and cook until caramelized. Place pineapple pieces and cherries into the doughnut pan and top with the caramel mixture.
3. **Bake Doughnuts:**
   Pour doughnut batter over the topping and bake at 350°F (175°C) for about 12-15 minutes.

Bourbon Glazed Doughnuts

Ingredients

For the Glaze:

- 1 cup powdered sugar
- 2 tablespoons bourbon
- 2 tablespoons heavy cream
- 1 teaspoon vanilla extract

Instructions

1. **Prepare and Fry Doughnuts:**
   Follow the Classic Doughnut recipe.
2. **Make the Bourbon Glaze:**
   Whisk powdered sugar, bourbon, heavy cream, and vanilla extract until smooth.
3. **Glaze Doughnuts:**
   Dip doughnuts into the bourbon glaze and allow it to set.

Cheesecake Doughnuts

Ingredients

For the Filling:

- 1 cup cream cheese, softened
- ¼ cup powdered sugar
- 1 teaspoon vanilla extract

For the Topping:

- Fresh fruit (strawberries, raspberries, or blueberries)

Instructions

1. **Prepare and Fry Doughnuts:**
   Follow the Classic Doughnut recipe.
2. **Make the Cheesecake Filling:**
   Mix cream cheese, powdered sugar, and vanilla extract until smooth.
3. **Fill Doughnuts:**
   Use a piping bag to fill doughnuts with the cheesecake mixture.
4. **Top Doughnuts:**
   Garnish with fresh fruit and a dusting of powdered sugar.

Dulce de Leche Doughnuts

Ingredients

For the Filling:

- 1 cup dulce de leche (store-bought or homemade)

For the Topping:

- 1 cup powdered sugar
- 2 tablespoons milk
- ½ teaspoon vanilla extract

Instructions

1. **Prepare and Fry Doughnuts:**
   Follow the Classic Doughnut recipe.
2. **Fill Doughnuts:**
   Use a piping bag to fill doughnuts with dulce de leche.
3. **Make the Glaze:**
   Whisk powdered sugar, milk, and vanilla extract until smooth.
4. **Top Doughnuts:**
   Drizzle the glaze over the filled doughnuts.

Chocolate Mint Doughnuts

Ingredients

For the Glaze:

- 1 cup powdered sugar
- 3 tablespoons cocoa powder
- 2 tablespoons milk
- 1 teaspoon peppermint extract

Instructions

1. **Prepare and Fry Doughnuts:**
   Follow the Classic Doughnut recipe.
2. **Make the Chocolate Mint Glaze:**
   Whisk powdered sugar, cocoa powder, milk, and peppermint extract until smooth.
3. **Glaze Doughnuts:**
   Dip doughnuts into the chocolate mint glaze and let it set.

Raspberry White Chocolate Doughnuts

Ingredients

For the Glaze:

- 1 cup powdered sugar
- 2 tablespoons raspberry puree
- 1 teaspoon lemon juice

For the Topping:

- ½ cup white chocolate chips, melted

Instructions

1. **Prepare and Fry Doughnuts:**
   Follow the Classic Doughnut recipe.
2. **Make the Raspberry Glaze:**
   Whisk powdered sugar, raspberry puree, and lemon juice until smooth.
3. **Glaze Doughnuts:**
   Dip doughnuts into the raspberry glaze and drizzle with melted white chocolate.